USING WILLS

Public Record Office
Pocket Guides to Family History

Getting Started in Family History

Using Birth, Marriage and Death Records

Using Census Returns

Using Wills

Using Army Records

Using Navy Records

USING WILLS

PUBLIC RECORD OFFICE

Public Record Office
Richmond
Surrey
TW9 4DU

ISBN 1 873162 90 1

A catalogue card for this book
is available from the British Library

Front cover: Professor Andrew Bruce Davidson,
24 February 1902 (PRO COPY 1/454)

Printed by Cromwell Press Ltd, Trowbridge, Wilts.

CONTENTS

INTRODUCTION

Unless you are lucky enough to find an old will amongst your family papers, your best chance of discovering one is among the records kept by the courts during the process of obtaining probate. These records go back to the fourteenth century: although the earliest ones are for wealthy people, they may give you the opportunity to go back a long way and to find out more about people's lives, families, worries and livelihoods. If you find a will, it can give you valuable detail about your family. This can help to fill gaps in your knowledge and open up fresh lines of research. Wills also give a deeper insight into family relationships and possessions than you can get from 'official' records.

Because there is the chance of going back a good way, and because wills change over time, you need to understand a bit about the background. Wills, in theory, had to be proved valid and probate granted by a court before any bequests could be paid. Before a will could legally be acted upon, a judge had to rule that it contained the last wishes of the deceased concerning the inheritance of his or her property and that those wishes were lawful. This process is called probate.

Searching for wills after 1858 is easy, as all wills in England and Wales were proved before a single court (with local branches), and a copy was kept in a central registry. They were well indexed, and the index has been published.

Before 1858, there were many courts, and although many of the wills have been indexed, you have the problem of knowing which court, and therefore which index, to look at. And, of course, the indexes aren't that easy to get at, and the records are scattered in lots of different record offices . . . It's a situation crying out for a new solution – a combined index of all wills before 1858, on computer, would help a lot!

This booklet explains what you are likely to find in a will. It explains the range of indexes available for searching, and how to use other types of record to help in your search. It tells you where the relevant records are held and how to make the best use of them. Before you set off on your search it is difficult to know which of these records will be of interest to you, and the wealth of material may seem daunting. Let your search lead the way, rather than trying to understand all the openings for research from the start.

MAKING WILLS

The making of formal wills which needed to be 'proved' in court was far from universal. Inheritance of land generally followed either the common law (eldest son gets all land, after the widow is taken care of; if there are no sons, daughters share all) or some local customary law (youngest son gets all land; all sons share equally). This kind of transfer of property from one generation to the next was

Probate jargon

testator/testatrix	the person whose will it is
executor/ executrix	the person responsible for having the will proved and then acting upon its provisions
intestate	a person who dies with estate to dispose of, but without making a will
administrator/ administratrix	a person appointed by the court to administer an intestate's estate
overseers	people appointed to ensure that the executor's job was properly done
inventory	a list of the deceased's property giving the value of individual items
life interest	when someone is given property during their lifetime only, with no power to sell or give it away
codicil	a later addition attached to a will changing or adding a clause

For a glossary of legal terms relating to probate, consult M. Scott, *Prerogative Court of Canterbury: Wills and Other Probate Records*.

already catered for by the law of the land. Inheritance of goods was the real subject of early wills, and it was the only area where the church courts (who granted probate before 1858) actually had any authority.

If your family was poor, and had little or nothing of value to pass on, there was no need to get a will proven in court. Will making has never been compulsory. If no will was left, the next of kin may only have gone to the trouble of seeking a grant of administration when there were complications such as debts, or if a dispute was likely. Many richer people also did not make wills for a variety of reasons. One common reason was because they were women. Married women did not in general have any control over their property while their husbands were alive, until the Married Women's Property Act 1882. Having said that, there is no need to assume that because your family was not rich they never made wills. People of all orders of society are represented among the will records, although the numbers of poor people fluctuates over time. The eighteenth century was apparently a period when fewer poor people made wills than either before or since.

Nowadays people tend to make their wills at the point when they acquire significant property, such as a house, or when they have children to pass their property on to. It is common for people to make changes to their wills several times as they get older. In the past, this was not often the way wills were made. It was not possible for people to

C 25 N

I Jane Austen of the Parish of Chawton do by this my last Will & Testament give and bequeath to my dearest Sister Cassandra Elizth everything of which I may die possessed, or which may be hereafter due to me, subject to the payment of my Funeral Expences, & to a Legacy of £50. to my Brother Henry, & £50. to Mde Bigeon — which I request may be paid as soon as convenient. And I appoint my said dear Sister the Executrix of this my last Will & Testament.

Jane Austen

April 27. 1817

The will of Jane Austen, April 27 1817
(PRO PROB 1/78, f.1)

plan their lives with any confidence. They were more likely to lose a spouse prematurely. They had less control over how many children they had and the likelihood of losing at least one child was much greater. There were also fewer systems and institutions in place to protect businesses and property. People were less likely to make a will at all, and if they did they would leave it as late as possible to avoid the unnecessary expense of making changes and to make sure that it was their final wishes that were acted upon.

It was not infrequent for people to leave making their wills so late that they had to be made orally in front of witnesses on the deathbed itself. These 'nuncupative' wills were written down at some point, but they were not signed or sealed by the person dying. Soldiers and sailors on active service generally made nuncupative wills. Nevertheless, if conducted properly, they were considered valid.

Apart from the very rich, most people's main concern was to pass on their housing and their land. In general, people had far fewer possessions of value than they do today and less disposable wealth. This was especially the case in the agriculturally based economy before the Industrial Revolution. A farmer's wealth was in the crops yielded by his land, and even after harvest he would probably not be rich in money terms since crops were usually either stored against the coming winter or exchanged by barter. What many people did have was land held by copyhold tenure – manorial land, held by 'copy of court roll'. In general, copyhold land could not be left by will until 1837, and so it was often not mentioned in the will.

How wills were made in the past

Noble and wealthy families with much to dispose of, and complicated arrangements to make, would have their wills drawn up by lawyers in much the same way as we would today. Ordinary people might not have access to a trained lawyer, and might well be illiterate. They would often call (sometimes at short notice) upon a known local figure with some experience of drawing up wills. This person would listen to the testator's wishes and would then go away to formulate them. There were several books available that gave model forms of wills, to be adapted for every occasion. The will would then be read out to the testator in front of witnesses and it would then be signed or sealed by testator and witnesses, assuming that the testator's wishes had been accurately noted.

Tradition, ritual and legal mystique grew up around will making. It became more than a formal list of property and how it was to be disposed of. It combined also a religious declaration and sometimes a leave-taking of the family. But very often the style of the will, if not the sentiments themselves, was that of the person who wrote it down rather than of the person whose property was being divided. Another important point to remember is that people were not by any means free to dispose of their property however they liked. The terms of a will had to be consistent with the laws governing property and the rights of the family over it, and there were strong traditions that were often followed, however unwillingly.

At first, in common with all other legal documents, wills were written in Latin. This was not the classical Latin still taught in some schools, but a medieval form, in which commonly used words and phrases were abbreviated. The use of English gradually increased so that by the 16th century very few wills were in Latin. But even then the judgments on probate, and probate clauses themselves, were in Latin, except between 1651 and 1660. Latin was abandoned altogether by an Act of Parliament in 1733.

Property covered in a will

The legal framework for property ownership was different to that in operation today, since all land was nominally under the control of the crown. This led to a legal division in the definition of property into real estate and personal estate. In the legal terminology of wills, the will dealt with the real estate and the testament with the personal estate, but by the 1850s this distinction was no longer being strictly observed.

Real estate

Real estate was land-based property, as opposed to 'personal' estate (goods and chattels). Real estate included land and buildings on it, together with the associated land rights. It might be held by freehold, which gave the holder the right to sell the property, or by copyhold, which was a type of tenancy where the land returned to the disposal of the lord of the manor at intervals.

When you are looking at a very old will you are unlikely to find a mention of the real estate. Certainly, if you do find no mention of real estate, it is not safe to assume that there was none. This is because real estate largely fell beyond the terms of the will. It had its own regulation through manorial courts and common law courts. The heir-at-law (usually the eldest son) would inherit the real estate automatically. Only from 1540 was disposal of some real estate by will approved by statute. From 1837 all kinds of real estate could be disposed by will.

Personal estate

Personal estate included leasehold houses and land, in which the lease covered a stated finite period. It also included personal effects, such as the contents of the household and any farm animals or equipment. It might also include debts due to or by the testator. Executors (or administrators if no will was left) had to be appointed by the probate court before debts could be collected by a law suit.

It is this type of property that wills were primarily dealing with. There was a great incentive to minimise the amount of personal estate bequeathed in a will since a duty on its value had to be paid to the Church. Nonconformists, of course, were particularly anxious to avoid this tax as far as possible.

Trusts

People also set up trusts to settle their property how they wished. The trustees would be bound by the wishes of the original holder of that property, often (but not always) expressed in the will. These were obviously very flexible, and could be used to protect property as well as the interests of dependants.

ⓘ Remember

Daughters would often have property settled on them when they were married, and this would not be mentioned in the will. It might then seem to the unwary that a daughter had been overlooked.

Likely contents of a will

The contents of many wills follow a set form, which might contain any of the main elements described below:

- **Preamble**. After 1858 wills usually begin 'This is the last will and testament of'. Before then, wills have a more religious tone, and usually begin 'In the name of God Amen' or 'In Dei Nomine Amen' in Latin followed by a declaration that the testator is of 'sound mind' and thus able to make a lawfully binding will. There is usually a formalised religious passage in which the testator commends his spirit to God. This passage may have been a standard form used by the person who wrote the will down, and not the words of the testator. It was probably not wildly different from his beliefs, though.

ⓘ Remember
The use of a phrase such as 'I hereby revoke all other wills' was required to make the will valid. It does not necessarily mean there was a previous will.

- **Charitable bequests.** These are very common, and can give clues to the place of origin of the testator.

- **Provision for the widow**. Older wills often refer to the widow's 'thirds', which means her legal entitlement to one third of her husband's real estate for life. Sometimes the wealthy would bequeath a sum of money instead of the 'thirds' so that the real estate could be left entirely in the hands of a son. Often, provision for a wife would have been established long before a will was made, and then there would be no need to mention what it was.

- **Provision for the children**. Usually the main house and the majority of any land went to the eldest son. This may well not be mentioned because legal provision for this was most commonly already written into the terms of ownership of both real estate and copyhold. Married daughters might also appear to have been overlooked – but their share of the estate might already have been given to them in the form of a dowry. In fact large inequalities in division of the property are more often a sign of funds already given than of disfavour.

- **Small bequests**. It was common to mention individually small items of monetary or sentimental value, such as jewellery or silver that was handed down from generation to generation. Small items or clothing were often given to loyal servants.

- **Remainder clause**. This was to avoid dispute about anything acquired after the will was made, and to make clear what should happen to any property not specifically mentioned.

ⓘ **Remember**
A person could lose a great deal of money between making a will and dying. Check the executor's records to find what was actually left.

What can you deduce from a will?

A will contains a great deal of straightforward information about a family, but there are also hidden clues within it that can help you in other branches of your research. You will often be able to tell from a will whether or not a daughter was already married at the time it was made. This might narrow down your search of the marriage records. There are also many possible inferences to be made about people's ages, which might help your search for a birth certificate.

> ### ⓘ Remember
>
> - The terms *father, brother* and *son, mother, sister* and *daughter* may be used to refer to in-laws as well as blood relatives.
>
> - The term *cousin* was used for all types of kin.

Omissions of family members from a will might indicate that they were already dead or that they were out of favour, but it is never safe to make assumptions of this type. Perhaps they had received their share of the family wealth already in a different way. Be careful not to read too much into what is there.

If you come across references to people who seem of significance but aren't connected to the family, it's a good tip to check out their wills as well. If you look, you may find a whole series of bequests to (or mentions of) your family that cast more light on their lives.

What if the person died intestate?

It was not infrequent for a man of property to die intestate (without making a will). Often the legal right of his wife or next of kin to inherit was clear and unchallenged, and there was therefore no recourse to law. If there was a possible challenge, his next of kin could apply for a grant of administration, to gain control over the estate.

Grants of administration were dealt with by the same courts, so they can be searched for broadly in the same way as wills. A record of any grant of administration was kept in a probate act book and a note was made in the probate register. There were also separate administration act books, in which a great amount of detail was given about the deceased and the next of kin.

The records of administrations have been compiled in different ways and appear in different formats. Many of the indexes have been published and can be searched at a number of libraries and record offices. Some of the will indexes listed below also include administrations.

SEARCHING FOR WILLS AND ADMINISTRATIONS AFTER 1858

On 12 January 1858 probate jurisdiction was taken away from the Church and moved to a new secular Court of Probate. In 1875 this probate court became part of the Supreme Court. This is excellent news for family historians, because the records were kept centrally, and are therefore easy to search. They were indexed each year (in some detail) in the *National Probate Register*, oaths of George Knight of Avon-street in the City and County aforesaid Coal Merchant and Henry Knight of Avon-street aforesaid Coal Merchant the Sons two of the Executors.

KNIGHT George.

Effects under £600.

24 December. The Will of George Knight late of Havant in the County of **Southampton** Builder deceased who died 18 May 1866 at Havant aforesaid was proved at **Winchester** by the oath of Mary Ann Knight of Havant aforesaid Widow the Relict the sole Executrix.

KNIGHT { George Browne Leak Esq.

Effects under £4,000.

1 August. The Will with two Codicils of George Browne Leak Knight late of Framingham Earl in the County of **Norfolk** Esquire deceased who died 18 June 1866 at Framingham Earl aforesaid was proved at **Norwich** by the oaths of Alfred Master of the City of Norwich Surgeon and the Reverend John Custance Leak of Plumstead in the County aforesaid Clerk the Brother two of the Executors.

KNIGHT Hannah.

Effects under £2,000.

15 November. The Will of Hannah Knight (Wife of John Knight) late of Farnworth in the County of **Lancaster** deceased who died 6 March 1866 at Farnworth aforesaid was proved at **Liverpool** by the oaths of James Collinge of Ashton-under-Lyne in the County aforesaid Surgeon and Apothecary the Brother and Charles Chorlton of the City of Manchester Stationer the Executors. Probate being granted under certain Limitations.

KNIGHT Henry.

Effects under £200.

4 August. Letters of Administration (with the Will annexed) of the Personal estate and effects of Henry Knight late of Dover in the County of **Kent** Bricklayer deceased who died 20 February 1832 at Dover aforesaid were granted at the **Principal Registry** to Rosina Knight of Dover aforesaid Spinster and Emily Knight of Dover aforesaid Spinster the Daughters and Executrixes of the Will of Sarah Knight Widow the Relict the sole Executrix and Universal Legatee named in the said Will of the said Deceased they having been first sworn.

KNIGHT Henry William.

Effects under £200.

21 April. The Will of Henry William Knight late of 8 Frederick-road Lorrimore-square Walworth in the County

10   x

A page from the *National Probate Register*

available on microfiche at lots of places (see p. 27). Remember that the year is that of the date of probate, not of death.

You can search the *National Probate Register* for free. Note the full name of the deceased, the date when probate or administration was granted, and the registry where the grant was made. For wills proved before 1931 in London you will need a note of the folio number (handwritten in the margin of the index). You need this information to request access to the will.

The information given in the indexes is enough in many cases to be sure that you have found the will you are looking for, without having to travel to London to check the original. Copies of wills and administrations can be ordered by post from the

▼ Court Service
  York Probate Sub-Registry
  Duncombe Place
  York YO1 2EA

The wills and letters of administration that were proved by the Court of Probate can be read at the Probate Searchroom in central London. No appointment is necessary but a fee is charged. A will requested and paid for by 3 p.m. can be seen on the same day, but go as early as possible because you will have to reorder the will on the next day if you need more time to read the detail.

▼ Probate Searchroom
Principal Registry of the Family Division
First Avenue House
42–9 High Holborn
London WC1V 6NP
Telephone: 020 7936 7000

Opening times (closed on bank holidays)

Monday to Friday   10.00 a.m. to 4.30 p.m.

What is in the indexes after 1858?

The indexes to wills proved from 1858 are organised separately by year when the will was proved. Within each year the testator's names are given in alphabetical order. Administration records are indexed together with probate records from 1871. The information given in the indexes for each testator until 1891 includes:

- name

- occupation

- address where the deceased lived when the will was made

- date and place of death

- marital status of women and the names of their husbands

- date of probate

- name of court that granted probate

- names, addresses and occupations of the executors, and their relationship to the deceased (if they were related)

- if a grant of administration was made, the name of the court that made the grant, the date when it was made and the name of the administrator

- valuation of the estate

After 1892 less detailed, but still considerable, information is given.

Copies of the indexes to wills made between 1858 and 1943 are widely available in London. Microform versions, often identified as the *National Probate Register*, are available at the Family Records Centre (FRC) and at the Public Record Office (PRO). They are also available at other libraries including the library of the Society of Genealogists. These copies may not contain all the handwritten annotations and folio numbers that are on the copies at the Probate Searchroom.

Outside London you may be able to find at least partial copies of the indexes in local record offices or libraries. There are District Probate Registries throughout England and Wales, where current probate business is carried out. These originally held copies of the national indexes but have usually relinquished them to local record offices because they cannot cater for historical research themselves.

Details of the whereabouts of these indexes are given in Gibson, *Probate Jurisdictions: Where to Look for Wills*. Your local library may have a copy of this indispensable and inexpensive directory, or you can buy it by post from the PRO bookshop. It is largely arranged by county, and then by church court within that, and gives you the date range of the surviving records, where they are kept, and details of any indexes.

For details of where to find your local record office see *Record Repositories in Great Britain*. Another possible way to consult the indexes locally is by arrangement at the Family History Centres of the Church of Jesus Christ of Latter-day Saints (see p. 32–3).

ⓘ Remember

It may be worth checking death duty records between 1858 and 1903: these can be detailed and they give the actual value of the estate. See p. 57–8.

Disputes over wills after 1858

After the Court of Probate was established in 1858, disputes over the validity of wills were heard there, with a right of appeal to the House of Lords. A dispute is indicated in the indexes to the records by a note of 'by decree' or 'former grant cessate'. You may find records of the actual judgements given in either the local registry or the local record office where the will was proved. The Public Record Office holds a sample of 7% of contentious cases in a collection (record class) called J 121.

If the dispute was about the content of the will rather than its validity, the case would have gone to the court of Chancery, and later the Chancery Division of the Supreme Court. The records of these courts are held by the Public Record Office. Many wills submitted as exhibits in court are in the class J 90, and these can be seen on three working days' notice.

SEARCHING FOR WILLS AND ADMINISTRATIONS BEFORE 1858

Until 1858 wills were proved and administrations granted in a network of church courts. The records are scattered across the country, and the search is therefore much harder. Many indexes have been published, but so far there is nothing that covers the whole range of courts involved. At first sight your search for a will might seem like looking for a needle in a haystack. (There is a 'shortcut' for the period 1793 to 1858 – the indexes to the death duty registers at the FRC and PRO give the court where a will was proved: see p. 57.)

The basic information you need to start investigating which court to look in is:

- a name
- an approximate date of death
- an approximate geographical area
- some idea of the status of the person or family you are looking for

Will indexes before 1858

Most wills have been indexed, and many of these indexes have been published, and can be seen in several places. Of course, the record office that holds the wills for a particular court will have indexes for that court, but it may not have other indexes for records held by other offices.

The indexes should give you a reference to the exact part of the large documents where a particular will is located. You can try to order copies by post from the relevant record office, citing the full reference from the index.

If the information you have about your ancestor is precise enough, in some record offices the staff will even conduct a brief search of their indexes for you, and send you a copy for a fee. In others (such as the Public Record Office), you may have to visit yourself, or employ an independent researcher.

Wills 1842

	Stewart	Elizabeth	Surrey	Apl	293
	Steer	William	Surrey	Apl	293
	Silvester	Maria	Oxford	Apl	293
	Shenton	James }			
		Richard }	Leicester	Apl	293
	Smith	Mary	Essex	Apl	293
	Siminton	Mary }			
		Elizabeth }	Middx	Apl	293
	Symmons	Richard	Dorset	Apl	293
	Seward	Francis	Devon	Apl	293
Esqr	Sherfield	James	Oxford	Apl	293
Esqr	Sherson	Robert	Middx	Apl	293
	Sims	Eliza }			
		Catherine	York	Apl	293
	Spiller	Robert	Devon	Apl	293
	Salter	Elizabeth	Stafford	Apl	293
	Swinton	George }			
		Alexander	Cambridge	Apl	293
	Shirley	Elizabeth	Kent	Apl	294
	Stowell	William			
		Stow	Durham	Apl	294
Esqr	Seton	George	North Brit.	Apl	294
	Spooner	Betty	Somerset	Apl	294
	Syms	John	Middx	Apl	294
	Swale	Thomas }			
		Steele }	York	Apl	294
	Sharpe	William	Kent	Apl	294
Esqr	Smith	William	Hereford	Apl	294

References to wills in the PROB 12 calendar for 1842
(PROB 12/251)

Indexes at the Society of Genealogists

The Society of Genealogists in London is probably the best place to search efficiently over a wide range of indexes. The library at the Society contains an extensive range of indexes to will records. It has published a directory of its holdings of will indexes, which is well worth consulting: this is Newington-Irving, *Will Indexes and Other Probate Material in the Library of the Society of Genealogists*. A small charge is made for visiting the library.

▼ Society of Genealogists
  14 Charterhouse Buildings
  Goswell Road
  London EC1M 7BA
  Telephone: 020 7251 8799
  Internet: http://www.sog.org.uk/

  Opening times (closed Sundays and Mondays)

Tuesday	10 a.m. to 6 p.m.
Wednesday	10 a.m. to 8 p.m.
Thursday	10 a.m. to 8 p.m.
Friday	10 a.m. to 6 p.m.
Saturday	10 a.m. to 6 p.m.

Indexes at the Family History Centres

Many of the indexes to wills that have been published, whether on paper or microfilm, can be consulted at the Family Record Centres of the Church of Jesus Christ of

Latter-day Saints (LDS). There are a number of these centres throughout the UK. You can find the one nearest you by contacting:

▼ The Genealogical Society of Utah
British Isles Family History Service Centre
185 Penns Lane
Sutton Coldfield
West Midlands B76 8JU

The indexes you require may have to be ordered in advance so you should make an appointment to do your search.

What church courts were there for probate?

People didn't have a free choice of where they got wills proved. The network of church courts was carefully graded. People with property in a local area only were dealt with locally; people with property that was slightly more scattered went to a regional court; and people with property scattered nationally went to the central courts of the Archbishops of York and Canterbury. There was also a property qualification for the central courts, of £5 in goods or land. This was very high when it was first set, but time and inflation drove this barrier down, and more people were able to use the central courts.

Where is the property?	Use this court	Where are the records?
All in one archdeaconry	Archdeacon's court (or possibly a 'peculiar court' with a very local jurisdiction)	Local record office
In more than one archdeaconry, but all in the same diocese	Bishop's diocesan court	Local record office
In more than one diocese	Archbishop's prerogative court	York – Borthwick Institute; Canterbury – Public Record Office or Family Records Centre

This system meant that wills bequeathing less property were proved locally, while the very wealthy, leaving complicated estates, had their wills proved under the supervision of an archbishop. There were two archbishop's courts with probate jurisdiction: the Prerogative Courts of Canterbury and York, covering different parts of the country as shown in the table on p. 36.

There were some instances in which this court hierarchy was overruled:

- If a will bequeathed personal property worth £5 (£10 in London) or more in both the north of England and the south or Wales, then it had to be proved in both archbishops' courts, first York and then Canterbury.

- If a person owning property in England or Wales (including soldiers and sailors) died overseas, the will was always proved in the Prerogative Court of Canterbury.

- During the English Civil War, there were two Prerogative Courts of Canterbury: one in Oxford, loyal to the King; and the other in London, loyal to Parliament.

- A separate Court for the Proving of Wills and Granting of Administrations had control over probate throughout England and Wales briefly during the Interregnum between 1653 and 1660. This was because the office of bishop had been abolished and the courts along with it. Many people avoided the expense of proving wills through this single court based far away in London by not bothering to have them proved at all. The records of this court are kept together with those of the Prerogative Court of Canterbury.

Archbishop's courts	Area covered
Prerogative Court of the Archbishop of York	York, Durham, Northumberland, Westmorland, Cumberland, Lancashire, Cheshire, Nottinghamshire and the Isle of Man
Prerogative Court of the Archbishop of Canterbury	South of England, Wales

Where are the wills before 1858 kept?

Most are now kept in local record offices. The records of the Archbishop of York's courts are kept at the Borthwick Institute, and those of the Archbishop of Canterbury's Prerogative Court are kept by the Public Record Office. (The Archbishop of Canterbury also had more local courts, whose records are kept at Canterbury.)

If you want to visit a record office, you should telephone first, to check what will records are held there and to make an appointment, if necessary.

Local record offices

Wills from the bishops' and archdeacons' courts are usually found in county record offices. You need to refer to Gibson's *Probate Jurisdictions: Where to Look for Wills* to find out which record office you should go to. For more information on that record office's location, opening times and so on, check in Gibson and Peskett, *Record Offices: How to Find Them*.

Prerogative Court of York

The records of the Prerogative Court of the Archbishop of York are held at the Borthwick Institute of Historical Research, in York. The collection of probate records available for searching here includes surviving records of all the courts with probate jurisdiction in Yorkshire from the 14th century to 1858. This excludes the period of the Interregnum, as explained above.

Microfilm copies of probate registers of the Prerogative Court of the Archbishop of York are available and the holdings of surviving original wills of the lesser courts are also on microfilm.

There is a variety of indexes available to help you research the holdings at the Borthwick Institute. Many have been published in the Yorkshire Archaeological Society Record Series, vols. 4, 6, 11, 14, 19, 22, 24, 26, 28, 32, 35, 49, 60, 73, 78, 89 and 93. If you cannot easily get to York you should be able to consult these in a library near you. Alternatively you can make use of the search service offered by the staff at the Institute. Searches are made for a fee charged per hour, with a minimum search time of 30 minutes.

You can also order copies of the probate records you find for a standard charge. Most documents can be photocopied, but any that are particularly fragile have to be photographed, which is more expensive. For administration records before 1690 you can request, for a small fee, a translated abstract (summary) from the entries in the probate books.

The Institute is open to members of the public who wish to do research. If you wish to visit the Institute, you should telephone in advance to make an appointment.

▶ Borthwick Institute
St Anthony's Hall
Peasholme Green
York YO1 7PW
Telephone: 01904 642315
Internet: http://www.york.ac.uk/inst/bihr/

Opening times (closed on bank holidays and for a week at Easter and for a longer period at Christmas).

Monday to Friday   9.30 a.m. to 12.50 a.m.
                             2.00 p.m. to 4.50 p.m.

Prerogative Court of the Archbishop of Canterbury (PCC), 1383–1858

This was the most senior church court in England. It was located in London rather than Canterbury. It was based in Doctors' Commons, by St Paul's Cathedral.

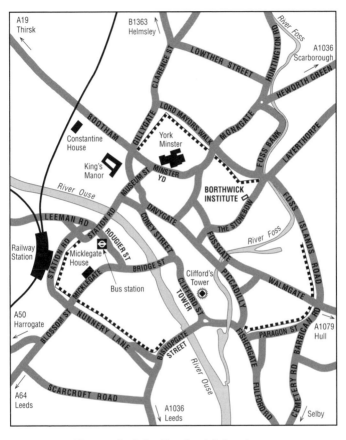

How to find the Borthwick Institute

During the 14th century there were few people with £5 or more to bequeath after their death, so the records of the court are very much weighted towards the rich. Over the succeeding centuries inflation moderated the effects of the £5 barrier, so that by the 19th century all ranks of society were represented in the records, and perhaps by the 1830s as many as a third of all wills made in England and Wales were proved in it. This makes its collected records the most important single source of information on wills. It has wills from 1383 to 1858, and administrations from 1559 to 1858.

PCC-registered wills and administrations can be seen at both the Family Records Centre and the Public Record Office. Other records of the PCC can only be seen at the Public Record Office.

What records did all these church courts compile?

Will records were compiled in these courts all over the country, in the order they were received for proving. The original will was handed to the court for proving. An exact copy was written out with the probate act attached. This was the executor's copy, and these have often ended up either in private hands, or in the records of law suits in the church or equity courts. The grant of probate was then entered in a probate act book. The original wills were also kept, though many have been lost. The executor could also pay for a copy of the will (and a note of the probate grant) to be made in the will register. This was the normal practice. This gives you four potential sources for information about a will proven before 1858:

- will registers
- probate act books
- probate copies of wills handed over to the executors
- original wills

SEARCHING THE RECORDS OF THE PREROGATIVE COURT OF CANTERBURY

The Public Record Office at Kew holds the records of the Prerogative Court of the Archbishop of Canterbury, 1383 to 1858. A selection of the most popular of these can also be seen on microfilm at the Family Records Centre. If you are just looking for a will or administration, and not for any further information, then the microfilms at the FRC are probably the best place to start.

In both locations, the records relating to wills and administrations are to be found under the PROB lettercode, where all the PRO's holdings from the Prerogative Court of Canterbury are held. The will registers are in the class (collection) PROB 11; administration records are in PROB 6.

At the FRC, as you come to each new class of records, you will find with it a laminated sheet of background information, which will act as a guide to understanding what you eventually find.

Visiting the Family Records Centre

▼ Family Records Centre
1 Myddelton Street
London EC1R 1UW
General telephone: 020 8392 5300
Telephone for birth, marriage and death certificates:
0151 471 4800
Fax: 020 8392 5307
Internet: http://www.pro.gov.uk/

Opening times (closed Sundays and Bank Holidays)

Monday	9 a.m. to 5 p.m.
Tuesday	10 a.m. to 7 p.m.
Wednesday	9 a.m. to 5 p.m.
Thursday	9 a.m. to 7 p.m.
Friday	9 a.m. to 5 p.m.
Saturday	9.30 a.m. to 5 p.m.

You can visit the FRC in person without an appointment at the opening times shown in the table. If you are unable to visit the FRC yourself you may want to consider employing a freelance researcher, as FRC staff cannot carry out searches on your behalf.

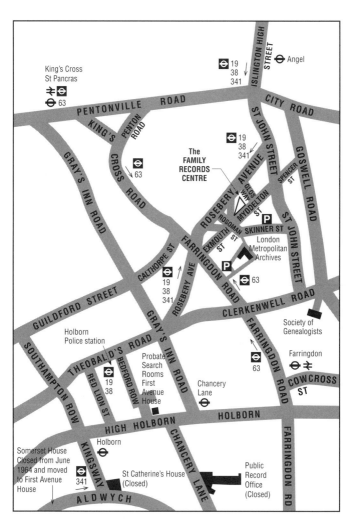

How to find the Family Records Centre

Visiting the Public Record Office

▼ Public Record Office
Kew
Richmond
Surrey TW9 4DU
General telephone: 020 8876 3444
Telephone number for enquiries: 020 8392 5200
Telephone number for advance ordering of documents
(with exact references only): 020 8392 5260
Internet: http://www.pro.gov.uk/

Opening times (closed Sundays and Bank Holidays)

Monday	9.00 a.m. to 5 p.m.
Tuesday	10 a.m. to 7 p.m.
Wednesday	9.00 a.m. to 5 p.m.
Thursday	9.00 a.m. to 7 p.m.
Friday	9.00 a.m. to 5 p.m.
Saturday	9.30 a.m. to 5 p.m.

No appointment is needed to visit the PRO in Kew, but you will need a reader's ticket to gain access to the research areas. To obtain a ticket you need to take with you a full UK driving licence or a UK banker's card or a passport if you are a British citizen, and your passport or national identity card if you are not a British citizen. Note that the last time for ordering documents is 4 p.m. on Mondays, Wednesdays and Fridays; 4.30 p.m. on Tuesdays and Thursdays, and 2.30 p.m. on Saturdays.

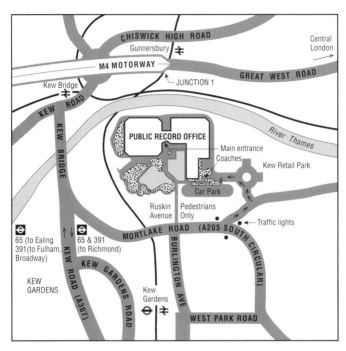

How to find the Public Record Office, Kew

Once you have your reader's ticket, you will need to go to the Microfilm Reading Room if you want to look for a will or administration, and to the Research Enquiries Room if you want to investigate some of the other records of the Prerogative Court of Canterbury (see pp. 52–5).

What to take with you to the PRO

- £1 coin (refundable) to leave any extra baggage in a locker

- money or a credit card if you are intending to buy copies of any records

- pencils (ink and rubbers are not allowed at Kew)

- paper to record what you find (notebooks are allowed, but no more than 6 loose sheets are permitted)

- a record of any research you have done so far

- a laptop computer if you wish

Indexes to PCC wills

There are many name indexes to the wills entered in the will registers (class PROB 11) at both the PRO and the FRC. You can also inspect them (with local will indexes) at the places mentioned pp. 30–33, 36–7.

Unfortunately they come from a variety of sources of variable quality, and have not been amalgamated. They therefore need to be approached separately and with patience. Because they have been created over many years, they often give an outdated reference, so that you need to translate the old reference into a new reference. The PRO is considering creating a cumulative computer index to get over these problems.

Converting the references

Before 1841, will registers in PROB 11 bear a name. The earliest will registers in PROB 11 generally cover several years and consist of only one volume. By the end of the sixteenth century the practice of confining each register to the wills and sentences registered in a single year had been established, and (with the growth in the Court's business) registers came to be made up of more than one volume. With the passage of time the number of volumes in a register increased, and by the mid-nineteenth century a single register might consist of twenty volumes.

Many of the indexes at the PRO, and older published sources, give you a reference based on the old register name. For example, looking for John Small in the index for 1649 gives the reference 64 Fairfax. This is composed of the name of the register and an internal quire number (see below). This is enough to order a copy by post.

To get the modern reference, you convert the register name to a PROB 11 reference by looking at the PROB 11 list. You then have to find the quire while looking at the register on microfilm.

These will registers each use a traditional numbering system, by quire instead of by page or folio. A quire consists of eight folios (i.e. sixteen pages). The quire number is *written* in roman or arabic numbers on the top left hand corner of the first page of the quire, and can be seen on the microfilm quite easily. An index entry is to the quire, and so may be to any of 16 pages within that particular quire: you just have to look through, using the details in the margin, to find the right will. When you have found it, take a note of the *stamped* folio number on the top of each right hand page. You will need this when using the self-service copiers. You can use either the quire number or the folio number to cite the document, but the folio number is more precise. Looking for John Small's will meant turning Fairfax into PROB 11/208, and quire 64 into folio 53.

Language and probate clauses

The texts of almost all wills proved were copied into large parchment registers, now seen on microfilm (PROB 11). The vast majority are in English; by the sixteenth century wills written in Latin are rare. Wills written in other modern European languages (usually Dutch and French) have an authenticated English translation. However, the probate clauses appended to the text of the wills, and the texts of sentences (judgements), are in Latin until 1733, with the exception of those in registers for 1651 to 1660, which are in English. They generally follow a standard form, however.

Buying copies

It is easy to make a copy of the microfilm version of a will both at the PRO and at the FRC. You can make them yourself for a small charge or ask staff to help you. If you want the staff to help you, take a note of the folio number stamped on the top of each right hand page of the will register you have been using. This gives an exact reference for the page number of the will you want copied. This is a particularly useful service for studying wills since they take some time to copy by hand and often contain a great deal of useful information that takes time to interpret. It is often easier to puzzle over such problems as unusual words, Latin abbreviations, obscure handwriting or strange omissions at leisure in your own home.

No will? What did administrators do?

If no will was left, next of kin or creditors could apply for letters of administration to be granted to them to settle the estate. Administrators were required to collect the credits owed to the intestate, and to pay the debts of the intestate and the expenses of the estate (such as medical fees, funeral bills and fees for the maintenance of dependants). The distribution of the estate after the payment of expenses and debts was regulated by statute and custom. One third of the estate was to be distributed to the wife of the intestate, and the remaining part was to be distributed in equal portions among the children.

Using the administration act books
The administration act books in PROB 6 have also been indexed, and the indexes are also available at the PRO, the FRC and the standard places (see pp. 30–33, 36–7). The act books do not usually give the complete texts of individual letters of administration. Rather, they record the information unique to individual letters. By far the majority of the entries in the administration act books take the form of brief formulaic summaries of the original grants. Except for the period 1651 to 1660, the act books are in Latin until 1733.

In some instances a grant was limited to a particular part of the deceased's estate, or special conditions were attached. Grants of the estates of soldiers and sailors limited to their wages were commonly made to creditors who had lent them money on the security of their wages.

OTHER PROBATE RECORDS AVAILABLE AT THE PUBLIC RECORD OFFICE

Only the most popular probate records are available at the FRC. For the rest, you have to go and consult the original documents at the PRO at Kew. There are many indexes available to help you.

Original wills

Most (but not all) PCC wills can be found in the registers of wills in PROB 11. Some people would not pay to have the will registered, and so you have to look in the so-called original wills, in PROB 10. You have to go to the PRO at Kew to see these, and you have to order them at least 3 days in advance of your visit, as they are stored off-site. They take 3 working days to be produced at Kew. Original wills survive in almost complete sequence from 1620; before that date an 'original will' may in fact be a facsimile copy made by the court. There is usually no advantage in looking at the original if there is a registered copy in PROB 11.

Not all wills were registered in PROB 11. Between 1383 and 1558 unregistered wills (now in PROB 10) are indicated in the index by the letter F. Genuine cases of unregistered wills, particularly after 1660, are very rare. If a calendar (a list of wills) or an index compiled from a calendar does not give a quire number alongside the name of a testator, it is sometimes assumed that the will was not registered and that therefore there is no copy of the will in PROB 11. However, in the majority of these cases, the registered text of the will can be found in the will register, by searching in the quires where you can find the wills of other testators whose surnames began with the same letter and whose wills were proved in the same months. In many other cases where no quire number is given, the whole entry in the calendar will be found to be a clerical error.

Wills of some famous people were extracted from the original wills now in PROB 10, and placed in PROB 1. Some supplementary series of wills, usually copies or rejected wills, may be found in PROB 20 to PROB 23.

Probate copies of wills, as handed over to the executors, often turn up as evidence in legal disputes: see pp. 30–33, 36–7.

Inventories and accounts

The executors or administrators had to prove to the court that they had carried out their functions properly. To do this, they had to submit inventories of the deceased's moveable property (including debts), and accounts of their expenditure (sometimes including expenditure on children over several years). This kind of probate record is relatively poorly used by family historians, despite the fact that there is a series of indexes to the relevant classes.

PCC lawsuits before 1858

In many cases, a will was disputed in the PCC. There are three main ways to discover if there was a dispute (a 'cause' in PCC language).

- The easiest way is to check the card index to the initial proceedings (1661–1858) in PROB 18. This is arranged in two parts, by name of cause (e.g. Smith *contra* Jones) and by name of the deceased, testator or intestate.

- There may be a clue in the will register in PROB 11. Until about 1800, a judgement may be entered in the margin next to the will, if the victorious party had paid for this to be done.

- If you go to the relevant act book (PROB 6 to PROB 9) or the PROB 12 calendar, you may find a marginal note saying *by decree* or *by sentence* (sometimes abbreviated). This means that the estate was the subject of a lawsuit or cause.

ⓘ Remember

Before the 18th century, causes were known by the name of the plaintiff, and not by the name of the person whose estate was being disputed.

The main classes to check are allegations (the initial complaint, by the plaintiffs) in PROB 18, answers by the defendants in PROB 25, depositions in PROB 24 and PROB 26, cause papers in PROB 28 and PROB 37, and exhibits in PROB 31 and PROB 36. Scott, in *Wills and Other Probate Records*, gives a step by step account of finding records in two testamentary disputes.

Other law suits in the PRO

Very many disputes over wills were heard not by the church courts (which dealt only with the validity of a will) but by the Court of Chancery. The records of this court are kept by the Public Record Office. An incomplete index, the Bernau Index, is available at the Society of Genealogists.

OTHER WILLS AT THE PUBLIC RECORD OFFICE, 13TH TO 20TH CENTURIES

Wills are found throughout the public records. Because some of them are individually described in the lists, it may be worth trying a keyword search in the PRO's on-line catalogue, using the surname and 'will' or 'probate' as the search terms. The on-line catalogue can be seen at Kew, or on the PRO website (at http://www.pro.gov.uk/).

Unfortunately, the on-line catalogue doesn't help with searching for wills in PROB 11!

There are many wills in Chancery Masters' Exhibits, C103 to C115. There is also a list of wills and related records in E 211.

The Paymaster General kept records of probates and letters of administration granted for Army and Navy personnel (it is not clear if they are for officers only) and their widows, between 1836 and 1915. The registers in PMG 50 can give clues to relationships, and the later ones give the address of the deceased.

Wills were deposited in the Navy Pay Office by naval ratings, Royal Marine other ranks and some warrant officers. The PRO at Kew has registers of the wills, 1786–1909, in ADM 142, which act as an index to the wills, 1786–1882, in ADM 48. There is also a very incomplete card index available. Wills of some army officers, 1755–1881, may be found in WO 42, and there is an index available at Kew. Wills and copies of wills may be found, very occasionally, among deceased soldiers' effects in the casualty returns, 1809–1910 (WO 25/1359–2410 and 3251–3471).

The probate records of the British Consular Court at Smyrna, Turkey, 1820–1929, and of the Shanghai Supreme Court, 1857–1941, are in FO 626 and FO 917 respectively. Other wills of some Britons in China, 1837–1951, are in FO 678/2729–2931.

DEATH DUTY RECORDS

Death duty records are the registers recording payment of taxes on the deceased's estate. Death duty has never been payable on very small estates, but the exact figure at which an estate became liable has varied at different times. Between 1796 and 1815 the duty was only levied on legacies given to people who were not close relatives of the deceased, so the number of estates incurring the duty was relatively small. After 1815 the scope of the duty was gradually widened so more people had to pay it. By 1857 every estate over the value of £20 lay within its scope. The registers were kept until 1903, when the system for recording payment was changed.

The main value of the death duty registers and their indexes, 1796–1858, to those who are researching wills is that they tell you the name of the court where probate or administration was granted. This can save you hours of searching through the will indexes.

The death duty registers also contain detailed information about the size of estates, which is not necessarily to be found in wills. They are an account of fact, rather than an aspiration about what might happen, which is what a will really is. In addition, annotations (notes) could be made on the registers for up to fifty years after the original probate or administration entry. These annotations yield valuable information about dates of death, subsequent marriages, changes of address and lawsuits disputing the will.

Death duty records were compiled according to the dates when probate or administration was granted. The records are held by the PRO in class IR 26 for the registers and IR 27 for the indexes. Microfilm copies of the indexes can be searched both at Kew and the FRC. The registers covering 1796 to 1857 can also be researched on microfilm at Kew and the FRC. The registers from 1858 to 1903 have not yet been filmed. They can be consulted only at Kew with advance notice of 3 working days.

WILLS MADE IN WALES

Many wills made in Wales were proved at the Prerogative Court of Canterbury. Records of those that were proved in the Welsh church courts are held at the National Library of Wales, Aberystwyth. These include the probate records of the church courts at:

- Bangor from 1635
- Brecon from 1543
- Chester from 1547 (Welsh wills only)
- Hawarden from 1554
- Llandaff from 1568
- St Asaph from 1565
- St David's from 1556

There is a computerised index available for searching these records.

ⓘ Remember
In border areas, if you can't find it in the Welsh records, a will might have been proved in the nearest English court. Try the records held at Hereford Record Office.

The National Library of Wales also holds register copy wills for the Welsh counties (except Montgomeryshire) from 1858 to 1941, together with a range of contemporary indexes to them. You can also research here the Calendar of Grants, 1858–1972. This is an annual index of all wills and grants of administrations in England and Wales.

You can order photocopies of original wills from the National Library of Wales by post if you can supply staff with a place of death and a fairly definite date of death or grant of probate.

▼ The National Library of Wales
  Aberystwyth
  Ceredigion SY23 3BU
  Telephone: 01970 632800
  Fax: 01970 632883
  Internet: http://www.llgc.org.uk/

Opening times (closed Sundays, Bank Holidays and first full week in October)

Monday	9.30 a.m. to 6 p.m.
Tuesday	9.30 a.m. to 6 p.m.
Wednesday	9.30 a.m. to 6 p.m.
Thursday	9.30 a.m. to 6 p.m.
Friday	9.30 a.m. to 6 p.m.
Saturday	9.30 a.m. to 5 p.m.

WILLS MADE IN SCOTLAND

The system and some of the traditions surrounding will making in Scotland were different to those in England and Wales. Scottish will records can be researched at the National Archives of Scotland. Records of wills and testaments made since the 16th century are held here.

Indexes to the wills records up to 1800 have been compiled and published by the Scottish Record Society. Copies of these can be consulted at libraries throughout the UK.

▼ National Archives of Scotland
  HM General Register House
  Edinburgh
  Scotland EH1 3YY
  Telephone: 0131 535 1314

Opening times (closed on bank holidays)

Monday to Friday   9.00 a.m. to 4.45 p.m.

WILLS MADE IN IRELAND

Irish wills were proved in the church courts of the archdiocese of Armagh. The surviving records have been divided between the two major archives for Ireland.

Northern Irish records

▼ Public Record Office of Northern Ireland
  66 Balmoral Avenue
  Belfast BT9 6NY
  Telephone: 028 9025 5905
  Internet: http://proni.nics.gov.uk/

Republic of Ireland records

▼ National Archives of Ireland
  Bishop Street
  Dublin 8
  Ireland
  Telephone: 00353 1 4072300
  Internet: http://www.nationalarchives.ie/

Most will records for Ireland made before 1904 were destroyed in a fire that devastated the Irish archives in

1922, though many of the indexes are available and can be consulted in libraries throughout the UK. The Society of Genealogists holds abstracts of Irish wills, 1569–1909.

<u>CONCLUSION</u>

This Pocket Guide provides an overview of how to locate and then use the various wills and probate records available. It should ensure that you start your search into this aspect of your family history fully armed with all the relevant tools and information! If this Pocket Guide has whetted your appetite for more information, a list of Further Reading is provided below.

FURTHER READING

A. J. Camp, *Wills and their Whereabouts* 4th ed. (London, 1974)

J. Cox, *Affection Defying the Power of Death: Wills, Probate and Death Duty Records* (FFHS, 1993)

J. Cox, *Hatred Pursued Beyond the Grave* (HMSO, 1993)

J. Gibson, *Probate Jurisdictions: Where to Look for Wills* 4th ed. (FFHS, 1997)

J.S.W. Gibson and P. Peskett, *Record Offices: How to Find Them* (FFHS, 1998)

N. Newington-Irving, *Will Indexes and Other Probate Material in the Library of the Society of Genealogists* (Society of Genealogists, 1996)

Record Repositories in Great Britain 11th ed. (PRO/ Royal Commission on Historical Manuscripts, 1999)

M. Scott, *Prerogative Court of Canterbury: Wills and Other Probate Records* (PRO, 1997)